# CONTENTS

# INTRODUCTION

The fighter plane is key to modern combat. Fast and easy to manoeuvre, it attacks enemies in the air. From the ground, the loops and rolls of the top guns are visible only as vapour trails.

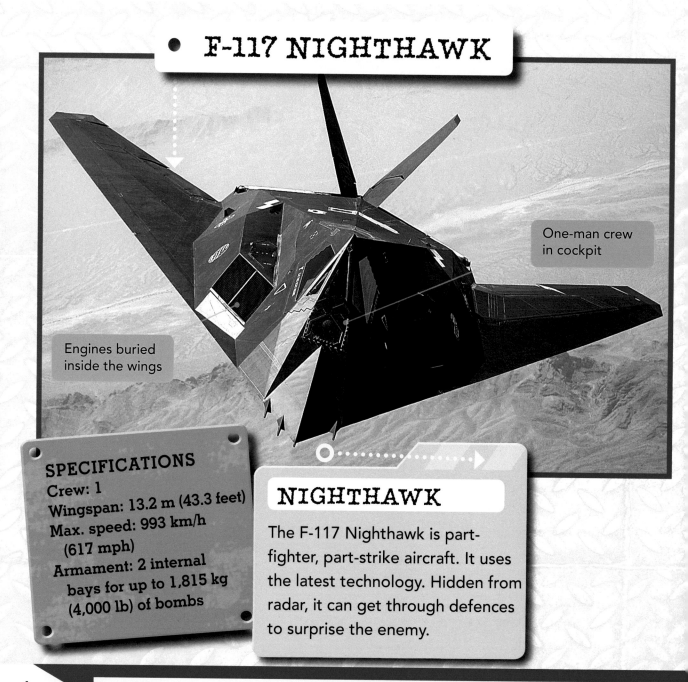

## F-117 NIGHTHAWK

One-man crew in cockpit

Engines buried inside the wings

### SPECIFICATIONS
Crew: 1
Wingspan: 13.2 m (43.3 feet)
Max. speed: 993 km/h
  (617 mph)
Armament: 2 internal
  bays for up to 1,815 kg
  (4,000 lb) of bombs

### NIGHTHAWK

The F-117 Nighthawk is part-fighter, part-strike aircraft. It uses the latest technology. Hidden from radar, it can get through defences to surprise the enemy.

RADAR: A system that uses radio waves to find the location of objects.

# ULTIMATE MILITARY MACHINES

# FIGHTER AIRCRAFT

Tim Cooke

WAYLAND
www.waylandbooks.co.uk

Published in paperback in Great Britain in 2018
by Wayland

Copyright © 2014 Brown Bear Books Ltd.

Wayland
An imprint of Hachette Children's Group
Part of Hodder & Stoughton
Carmelite House
50 Victoria Embankment
London EC4Y 0DZ
An Hachette UK Company
www.hachette.co.uk
www.hachettechildrens.co.uk

All Rights Reserved.

Dewey Number: 623.7'464-dc23
ISBN: 978 1 5263 0538 1
10 9 8 7 6 5 4 3 2 1

Brown Bear Books Ltd.
First Floor
9–17 St. Albans Place
London
N1 0NX

Managing Editor: Tim Cooke
Picture Manager: Sophie Mortimer
Art Director: Jeni Child
Editorial Director: Lindsey Lowe
Children's Publisher: Anne O'Daly
Production Consultant: Alastair Gourlay

Printed in China

Picture Credits

Key: t = top, c = centre, b = bottom, l = left, r = right.

Front Cover: U.S. Airforce

BAe Sytems: 28tr; John Batchelor: 06/07; Bundesheer:
29br; Coert van Breda: 27tc; Corel: 05bl; Robert Hunt
Library: 05tr, 06bl, 08, 17tl, 17cr, 20, 21; U.S. Airforce:
04, 06cl, 09bl, 09br, 11cl, 11bl, 13tr, 14c, 22tc, 27bl;
U.S. Department of Defense: 07br, 10, 11tr, 12/13,
13bl, 14br, 15b, 16, 18/19, 18b, 19b, 22br, 23, 24,
25tr, 25b, 26bl, 28bl; U.S. Marine Corps: 09tl, 15tr;
U.S. Navy: 17bl, 26tr, 29tr.

All Artworks: Brown Bear Books.

Brown Bear Books Ltd. has made every effort to trace
copyright holders of the pictures used in this book.
Anyone having claims to ownership not identified above
is invited to contact: licensing@brownbearbooks.co.uk

Websites
The website addresses (URLs) included in this book
were valid at the time of going to press. However,
because of the nature of the internet, it is possible that
some addresses may have changed, or sites may have
changed or closed down since publication. While the
author and publisher regret any inconvenience this may
cause the readers, no responsibility for any such changes
can be accepted by either the author or the publisher.

# EARLY DAYS

Early in World War I, both sides used aeroplanes for observation. Aircraft flew over enemy positions. But military planners could already see their potential as weapons.

▲ A squadron of U.S. Army World War I biplanes (planes with two sets of wings). Pilots who shot down many enemy fighters were called 'aces'.

# WORLD WAR I

In World War I (1914–1918), scout aircraft flew above the trenches to spy on the enemy. Each carried a pilot and an observer. To begin with, the observers fired rifles at any enemy scouts. Soon, the aircraft were fitted with machine guns.

# WORLD WAR II

At the start of World War II (1939–1945), Germany used blitzkrieg tactics to conquer much of Europe. Ju 87 Stuka dive bombers and Heinkel 111s struck airfields and cities. Blitzkrieg tactics depended on quickly winning control of the skies to dominate the enemy.

◀ A British Spitfire (top) and a German Me 109. These planes fought in the Battle of Britain in 1940.

BLITZKRIEG: A German word that means 'lightning war'.

# WHAT IS A FIGHTER?

A fighter is a military aeroplane designed to destroy the enemy in the air. Fighters are lightning fast and easy to turn in tight twists or loops. Modern fighters carry a combination of machine guns, rockets and missiles. They also use bombs to strike targets on the ground.

## F-16 FIGHTING FALCON

◄ An F-16 Fighting Falcon fires an AIM-120 air-to-air missile. A fighter's main job is to destroy enemy fighters.

## AERIAL DUEL

Vapour shows the trail of enemy fighters in a dogfight in World War II. Each pilot tried to get the other in his sights to shoot at while not getting shot down himself.

Four cannon mounted in nose

DOGFIGHT: A one-on-one, close-range clash between two fighters.

# FIRST FIGHTER

World War II saw a race for fighter power. Late in the war, Germany produced the Messerschmitt Me 262. It was the first jet fighter. It could fly higher and faster and climb more quickly than propeller-driven planes. But it came too late to change the outcome of the war.

Swastika, symbol of the Nazis

ME 262

Aerodynamic cockpit canopy

Swept-back wings increase speed

Jet engines draw air into turbines

▶ U.S. F-16 Fighting Falcons fly in formation. Formations allow fighters to protect one another from attack.

**AERODYNAMIC:** Designed so that air passes easily over a surface.

# FIGHTER ROLE

A fighter's traditional job has been to defend airspace. Its key method of defence is attack. It strikes enemy aircraft before they can gain air superiority. Today, fighters often have both defensive and offensive roles. They are called multi-role combat aircraft (MRCA).

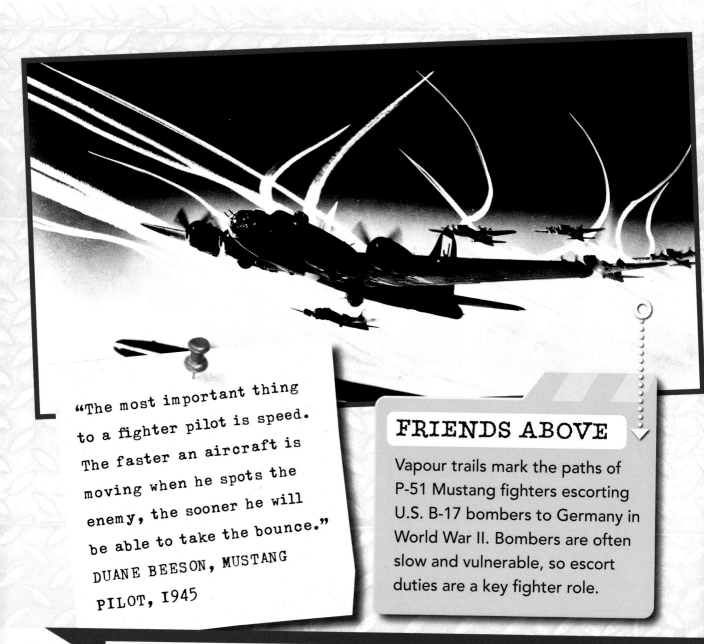

"The most important thing to a fighter pilot is speed. The faster an aircraft is moving when he spots the enemy, the sooner he will be able to take the bounce."
DUANE BEESON, MUSTANG PILOT, 1945

## FRIENDS ABOVE

Vapour trails mark the paths of P-51 Mustang fighters escorting U.S. B-17 bombers to Germany in World War II. Bombers are often slow and vulnerable, so escort duties are a key fighter role.

8

TAKE THE BOUNCE: To get out of a situation.

## SOUND BARRIER

Vapour created by water from the atmosphere bursts around a U.S. Navy F/A-18 Hornet as it breaks the sound barrier. Whatever weapons a fighter plane carries, its greatest weapon is still sheer speed.

"The first time I ever saw a jet, I shot it down."
CHUCK YEAGER, UNITED STATES AIR FORCE, ON MEETING AN ME 262.

## SOUND AND BEYOND

The key part of a modern air force is the supersonic fighter, faster than the speed of sound. Modern MRCAs are highly adaptable. They are used in air-to-air combat, or for ground attack or bombing tasks.

▲ U.S. pilot Chuck Yeager was the first man to break the sound barrier, in 1947. The U.S. soon began using supersonic fighters (left).

SOUND BARRIER: The speed of sound, or 1,235 km/h (768 mph).

# AIRBORNE POLICE

In times of threat, the Combat Air Patrol (CAP) gets off the ground. Its fighters look out for enemy intruders as a first line of defence. CAPs are common over areas where war seems imminent.

## F-15 EAGLE

### EAGLE EYES

The F-15 Eagle is a tactical fighter. Its main job is to take out enemy aircraft and command centres. The pilot uses a heads-up visual display to aim guns and missiles.

▲ Two U.S. F-15s and an AT-38 (centre) fly on CAP over the desert in the Persian Gulf in the 1990s.

**HEADS-UP VISUAL DISPLAY:** A visor that displays information.

# PROTECTING THE PEOPLE

Fighters guard against air terror. In the attacks of 11 September 2001, terrorists used aircraft to attack New York City and Washington, DC. Under Operation Noble Eagle, fighters now patrol the skies 24 hours a day, protecting the United States.

▼ F-15 Eagles fly a CAP over the eastern seaboard of the United States.

## F-117 NIGHTHAWK

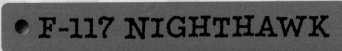

## NOBLE EAGLE

## SIGHT UNSEEN

The F-117 Nighthawk is an attack fighter that was first flown in 1981. The stealthy Nighthawk can strike its targets without ever being 'seen' by enemy radar.

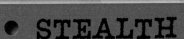

## STEALTH

◀ The exterior of the Nighthawk is coated with a secret non-reflective material and flown with computerised controls.

NON-REFLECTIVE: Material that does not bounce back radar signals.

# FIGHTER FIREPOWER

The fighter plane is a hunter. It locates enemy aircraft and destroys them. At long range, modern planes use missiles; in close combat, cannons do the job. Fighter–bombers that are designed to strike ground targets carry air-to-ground missiles and bombs.

## FULLY LOADED

The F-16 Fighting Falcon carries wingtip and rack missiles. The fighter was built to be unstable as it flies. It bounces around in the air, which actually makes it easier to manoeuvre.

## SPECIFICATIONS

Crew: 1
Wingspan: 9.96 m (32.6 feet)
Max. speed: 2,410 km/h
(1,500 mph)
Armament: 1 cannon,
4 rocket, 4–6 missiles,
8 bombs

## ● F-16 FIGHTING FALCON

Fire-control radar in nose finds targets

Air intake for engine

CANNON: An automatic, heavy gun carried by an aircraft or tank.

## GUIDANCE

Firing is not left to chance. Precision-guided missiles (PGMs) lock onto another aircraft, no matter how it tries to dodge. The precision systems work by radar or infrared technology.

## SIDEWINDER

The Sidewinder air interception missile (AIM) is guided by infrared. It has a range of up to 18 km (11 miles). It is still one of the most effective short-range missiles.

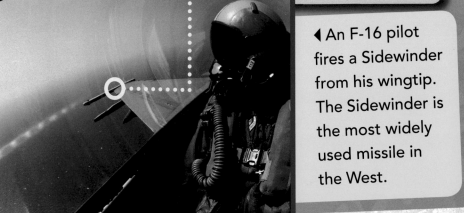

◀ An F-16 pilot fires a Sidewinder from his wingtip. The Sidewinder is the most widely used missile in the West.

Wing rack for rockets

**INFRARED:** Invisible waves, usually generated by heat.

# FIGHTER BOMBERS

MRCAs are not just designed to fight other aircraft. They can also strike targets on the ground. Aircraft like the F-16 Fighting Falcon carry guided missiles and bombs. The weapons are steered by laser or by video via the pilot's screen.

## MAVERICK

An F-16 launches a Maverick air-to-ground missile. The missile's on-board camera is linked to a video screen in the cockpit. The pilot steers the missile to its target.

## • F-16 MISSILE

## LASER ROCKET

An F-15 Eagle drops heat-seeking rockets. Sensors in the rockets' noses guide them precisely to their targets.

COCKPIT: The part of an aircraft where the pilot sits.

# GUNS AND CANNON

Modern fighters often carry high-speed 20 mm Gatling guns. They are designed for close-range combat, so are rarely used. Modern air warfare is fought at longer range, so pilots rely more on missiles.

"In combat flying, precision aerobatic work is really not of much use. It is the rough manoeuvre that succeeds."
'BUBI' HARTMANN, GERMAN ACE, WWII

## WORLD WAR II ACE

American pilot Gregory 'Pappy' Boyington shot down at least 22 enemy planes in World War II. He was the Marine Corps' top-scoring ace in the conflict. He later led the famous Black Sheep Squadron.

## ● P-47 THUNDERBOLT

▲ A P-47 Thunderbolt fires its wing guns at night in World War II.

GATLING GUN: A machine gun with multiple rotating barrels.

# FIGHTER CREW

From World War I aces to today's high-tech aircrew, pilots have been seen as lone warriors high above the earth. But in modern conflict, teamwork and co-ordination between the air and the ground are vital.

## TEAM AT WORK

A modern fighter cockpit is a communications centre. Pilots talk constantly to air controllers or with other pilots on the same mission. Wherever they are, fighter pilots are never alone.

## G-SUITS

For high-altitude, high-speed combat, fighter pilots wear heated G-suits. The suits have built-in features to prevent loss of blood from the head during fast combat moves.

**G-SUIT:** Overalls designed to resist the effects of gravity (g-force or 'G').

## WORLD WAR I

In World War I, fighter cockpits were open to the weather. Pilots wore fur-lined leather coats for warmth. Their heads and eyes were protected by a tight leather helmet and goggles.

## WORLD WAR II

Although cockpits in World War II were enclosed, pilots still wore thick clothes against the cold. They often wore life jackets, in case they had to ditch at sea.

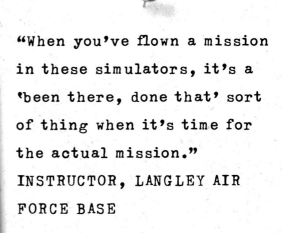

## VIRTUAL REALITY

Modern pilots train in simulators. They can practice manoeuvres or fight the enemy above accurate images of real landscapes.

"When you've flown a mission in these simulators, it's a 'been there, done that' sort of thing when it's time for the actual mission."
INSTRUCTOR, LANGLEY AIR FORCE BASE

DITCH: To crash-land an aircraft at sea.

# FIGHTER TACTICS

The skill of a pilot under pressure determines how well a fighter plane performs. To make sure a pilot is always at his best, pilots train and practice continually. Some of the combat tactics they use have not changed since World War I.

"The duty of the fighter pilot is to patrol his area of the sky, and shoot down any enemy fighters in that area."
MANFRED VON RICHTHOFEN, GERMAN ACE, 1917

## COMBAT RULES

Since World War I, a pilot has learned three basic rules: to attack from above and behind; to keep watching the sky; and to guard against attacks out of the sun.

**FIRE CONTROL:** Systems that keep guns and missiles locked on target.

◀ F-16s have powerful fire control radars that map the ground and can lock on to up to 10 targets at a time.

## ELECTRONICS

In modern warfare pilots rely on the latest technology to seek out and hit a target while in flight. The enemy can be out of sight but radar will locate him. The pilot can then activate guided missiles that lock-on. They travel at Mach 4 – up to four times faster than the speed of sound, or about 4,000 km/h (2,500 mph).

## WINGMAN

A pilot's best friend is his wingman. The wingman flies behind and to the side of the lead aircraft. His job is to protect the leader from enemy coming in from behind or from the side.

▲ Three U.S. F-15s fly in a V-shape. This formation allows the lead jet to seek out enemy targets, while the other aircraft protect it from flank attacks.

LOCK-ON: When a missile is fixed on its target and guided toward it.

# FIGHTER HISTORY

Since the early fighter planes of World War I, many things have changed in fighter technology: the planes, the training, the missiles and the equipment. But the job remains the same – to destroy enemy aircraft and to defend the skies.

## MUSTANG MARVEL

The North American P-51 Mustang was one of the star performers of World War II, helping to defeat the Luftwaffe. The long-range escort fighters protected Allied bombers on raids over Germany. They cut casualties among the heavy bombers.

### SPECIFICATIONS
Crew: 1
Wingspan: 11.3 m (37 feet)
Max. speed: 702 km/h
  (437 mph)
Ceiling: 12,800 m (42,000 feet)
Armament: 6 x 0.5-inch
  Browning machine guns

LUFTWAFFE: The name of the German Air Force.

## WORLD WAR II

The early U.S. bombers that flew over Germany were slow and easy targets for fast German fighters. The P-51 Mustang changed that. It was fast and could fly at high altitudes, making it an ideal escort fighter.

## ANTI-AIRCRAFT

Anti-aircraft artillery provides the best defence against low-flying fighter-bomber attacks. Here, U.S. Marines fire on Japanese fighters during World War II.

"We soon found out that the P-51 Mustang was indeed a different breed of aircraft. It was fast, for one thing..."
ROBERT GOEBEL, GERMAN FIGHTER PILOT

## JOHN GLENN, JR.

American John H. Glenn, Jr., the first astronaut to orbit the Earth, was a fighter pilot in World War II and Korea (1950–1953). He won many medals for bravery, shooting down three MiGs.

MIG: A Russian-built fighter plane.

# KOREAN WAR

During the Korean War (1950–1953), jet fighters were used for the first time. U.S. F-86 Sabres, backing the United Nations and South Korea, fought Soviet-built MiG-15s, supporting North Korea, to control part of the sky known as 'MiG Alley'.

▼ John Glenn's F-86 Sabre in Korea carried the words 'MiG Mad Marine'. Glenn shot down three MiGs.

● F-86 SABRE

## AIR SUPREMACY

After Korea, the U.S. developed the F-105 Thunderchief. This fighter-bomber was used extensively in the Vietnam War.

**UNITED NATIONS:** An organisation set up to resolve international disputes

# LIBYA

In 1981, Libya's then-leader Muammar al-Qaddafi announced that he wanted to extend Libyan territory up to 19 km (12 miles) into the Mediterranean Sea. That would have broken international law. U.S. aircraft carriers were sent to stop the Libyan advance.

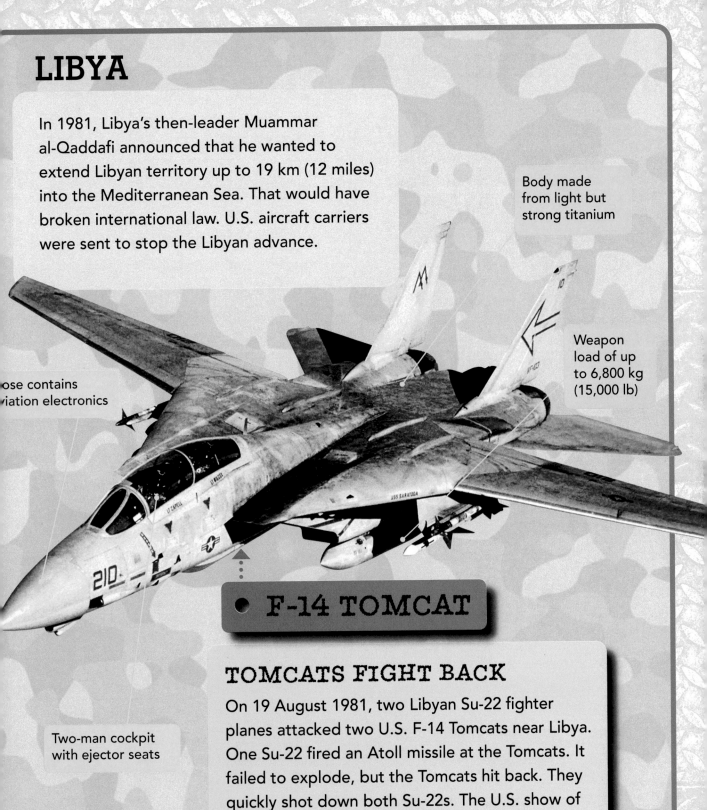

Body made from light but strong titanium

Weapon load of up to 6,800 kg (15,000 lb)

ose contains viation electronics

Two-man cockpit with ejector seats

F-14 TOMCAT

## TOMCATS FIGHT BACK

On 19 August 1981, two Libyan Su-22 fighter planes attacked two U.S. F-14 Tomcats near Libya. One Su-22 fired an Atoll missile at the Tomcats. It failed to explode, but the Tomcats hit back. They quickly shot down both Su-22s. The U.S. show of aerial strength meant that Libya could not carry out the planned extension of its borders.

**EJECTOR SEAT:** A safety seat that propels a pilot out of a plane.

# FALKLANDS WAR

In April 1982, Argentina occupied the British-owned Falkland Islands, just off the Argentine coast. The British sent a naval task force to the South Atlantic. Hawker Sea Harriers destroyed at least 20 enemy fighters and established air superiority. That allowed an amphibious landing to take place. The Argentines surrendered after two-and-a-half months' fighting.

▼ The British Hawker Sea Harrier served in the Falklands War, both Gulf Wars and the Balkans conflict in the 1990s.

## SEA HARRIER

The British only had one fighter plane capable of flying from the Royal Navy's V/STOL carriers: the Hawker Sea Harrier. In the Falklands War, British pilots flew 1,435 missions with no losses.

V/STOL: Vertical/short take-off and landing.

# DESERT STORM

During the 1991 Gulf War, Coalition forces fought back against the Iraqi invasion of neighbouring Kuwait. Fighter aircraft led by the United States carried out more than 100,000 sorties. They targeted the military capabilities of the enemy.

▲ A U.S. F-16 leaves its base in Europe in 2011 to take up position in Iraq.

## MIG DOWN

A MiG fighter lies in ruins after being shot down during the first Gulf War. Russian-built MiGs were used extensively by the Iraqis, but were slow and easy to attack.

SORTIE: A word used to describe an individual military flight or mission.

25

# GALLERY

Fighter planes are extremely fast and relatively small, with only one or two crew members. They are the best defence any air force can have. They can destroy an enemy from long range.

## F-35 LIGHTNING II

### SPECIFICATIONS
Crew: 1
Wingspan: 10.7 m (35 feet)
Max. speed: 1,930 km/h
(1,200 mph)
Armament: 4-barrel
Gatling cannon

The F-35 is becoming the most important multi-role fighter of the U.S. Air Force. It offers ground attack, air defence and reconnaissance.

## F-117 NIGHTHAWK

The F-117 was a ground-attack aircraft built in the 1980s. It was the first fighter to use stealth technology. Only 59 went into service.

### SPECIFICATIONS
Crew: 1
Wingspan: 13.2 m (43.3 feet)
Max. speed: 993 km/h (617 mph)
Armament: 2 bombs, including
nuclear bombs

RECONNAISSANCE: Secretly gathering information about the enemy.

## MIG-29 FULCRUM

### SPECIFICATIONS
Crew: 1
Wingspan: 11.4 m (37½ feet)
Max. speed: 2,400 km/h
(1,490 mph)
Armament: 1 x 30 mm
cannon; up to 3,500 kg
(7,720 lb) of ordnance

The MiG-29 Fulcrum is the fourth generation of Russian-built all-weather fighters. In service since 1983, it is the equivalent of the U.S. F-15 and the U.S. F/A-18. It is widely used around the world.

## F-22 RAPTOR

### SPECIFICATIONS
Crew: 1
Wingspan: 13.56 m
(44½ feet)
Max. speed: 2,410 km/h
(1,500 mph)
Armament: 6-barrel
Gatling cannon

The Raptor entered service in 2005. The fighter uses stealth technology and is suited to ground-attack or electronic warfare roles, as well as air-to-air combat.

**ORDNANCE:** Shells and other ammunition carried by an aircraft.

# GALLERY

## MIRAGE 2000

The Dassault-Breguet Mirage 2000 is a multi-role, single-engine jet fighter used by the French Air Force. It has seen action in the Gulf Wars, Bosnia and Kosovo. In 2011, it was used to enforce a no-fly zone over Libya.

**SPECIFICATIONS**
Crew: 1
Wingspan: 9.13 m (29 feet)
Max. speed: 2,530+ km/h (1,500+ mph)
Armament: 2 x 30 mm revolver cannon; up to 4000 kg (8,820 lb) ordnance

## GR4 TORNADO

**SPECIFICATIONS**
Crew: 2
Wingspan: 13.99 m (46 feet)
Max. speed: 2,400 km/h (1,490 mph)
Armament: 1 x 27 mm revolver cannon; up to 9,000 kg (19,800 lb) payload

The Tornado is a multi-role British fighter. The angle of its wing sweep can be varied by the pilot for maximum performance.

**NO-FLY ZONE:** An area over which aircraft are forbidden to fly.

The French-built Rafale 169 is a multi-role fighter. It was used during the Libyan Civil War of 2011 to enforce the United Nations' no-fly zone.

## RAFALE 169

### SPECIFICATIONS
Crew: 1 or 2
Wingspan: 10.8 m (35½ feet)
Max. speed: 2,130 km/h
  (1,324 mph)
Armament: 1 x 30 mm
  cannon; up to 9,500 kg
  (21,000 lb) ordnance

## EUROFIGHTER

### SPECIFICATIONS
Crew: 1 or 2
Wingspan: 10.9 m
  (35 feet 8 inches)
Max. speed: 2,495 km/h
  (1,550 mph)
Armament: 1 x 27 mm
  revolver cannon; up to
  7,500 kg (16,500 lb) payload

The Eurofighter is a multi-role fighter that was developed jointly by several European air forces. It has been in use since 2003.

PAYLOAD: How much an aircraft can carry in addition to its crew.

# GLOSSARY

**aerodynamic** Designed so that air passes easily over a surface.

**airspace** The part of the sky above a particular country.

**amphibious** Operating on land and on water.

**anti-aircraft artillery** Large guns such as cannon used to fire at aircraft.

**blitzkrieg** A German word that means 'lightning war'.

**cannon** An automatic, heavy gun carried by an aircraft or tank.

**cockpit** The part of an aircraft where the pilot sits.

**ditch** To crash-land an aircraft at sea.

**dogfight** A one-on-one, close-range clash between two fighter planes.

**ejector seat** A seat with a parachute that lifts a pilot out of a plane.

**fire control** Systems that keep guns and missiles locked on target.

**Gatling gun** A machine gun with multiple rotating barrels.

**G-suit** Overalls designed to resist the effects of high gravity ('G' forces).

**heads-up visual display** A visor that displays information.

**infrared** Invisible waves, usually generated by heat.

**lock-on** When a missile is fixed on its target and guided towards it.

**Luftwaffe** The name of the German Air Force during World War II.

**MiG** A Russian-built fighter plane.

**no-fly zone** An area over which aircraft are forbidden to fly.

**non-reflective** Material that does not bounce back radar signals.

**ordnance** Shells and other ammunition carried by an aircraft.

**payload** How much an aircraft can carry in addition to its crew.

**radar** A system that uses radio waves to find the location of objects.

**reconnaissance** Secretly gathering information about the enemy.

**sortie** A word used to describe an individual military flight or mission.

**sound barrier** The speed of sound, 1,235 km/h (768 mph).

**superiority** A situation in which one side has a clear advantage over another.

**UN** The United Nations, an organisation set up to resolve international disputes.

**vapour** The speed of sound, 1,235 km/h (768 mph).

**visual display** A helmet with a visor that displays information.

**V/STOL** Vertical/short take-off and landing.

# FURTHER READING

## BOOKS

Brook, Henry. *Fighter Planes* (Usborne Beginners Plus). Usborne, 2012.

Clements, Gillian. *Great Events: The Battle Of Britain.* Franklin Watts, 2004.

Gilpin, Daniel. *Machines Close-up: Modern Military Aircraft.* Wayland, 2009.

Graham, Ian. *Attack Fighters.* Heinemann Library, 2003.

Rickard, Stephen. *Fighter Pilot (321 Go!).* Ransom Publishing, 2010.

Nagelhout, Ryan. *Fighter Planes (Mighty Military Machines).* Gareth Stevens Publishing, 2015.

Zuehlke, Jeffrey. *Fighter Planes* (Pull Ahead Books) Lerner Publications, 2005.

## WEBSITES

**http://www.sr-71.org/aircraft**
Military aircraft information gallery with images and fact sheets.

**www.military.com/video/aircraft/jet-fighters**
Videos of fighter planes in action.

**http://www.toptenz.net/top-10-fastest-military-airplanes.php**
Videos of the world's Top 10 fastest fighter planes.

**http://science.howstuffworks.com/wwii-plane.htm**
Howstuffworks page about fighter aircraft in World War II.

**http://www.combataircraft.com/en/Military-Aircraft/fighter-attack/**
Comprehensive guide to fighter and attack aircraft.

**www.fighter-planes.com**
Technical data and photographs.

# INDEX